Sweet Communion

SHARISSE ARNOLD

authorHOUSE®

AuthorHouse™
1663 Liberty Drive
Bloomington, IN 47403
www.authorhouse.com
Phone: 1 (800) 839-8640

Published by AuthorHouse 02/17/2016

ISBN: 978-1-5049-7996-2 (sc)
ISBN: 978-1-5049-7995-5 (e)

Print information available on the last page.

Acknowledgements

May those who encouraged, prodded and held fast to their love with me know just how deeply I appreciate you all!

In times of apprehension and discouragement I had the best of people join up and inspire me to not give up on the dream God birthed within me:

Debra Robinson (my beautiful mom), Marilee Muse, Pat Sipes, Maryanne Green & Chiquita P. Jones *(I'm not Afraid to Talk about It)* – your urging, confidence and reassurance that *Sweet Communion* needed to be in print for others outside of just who I knew.

Brandon, Elaney and Kinlee – for being the best husband and daughters anyone could ever ask for. Thank you for your understanding and love.

I love you all deeply and dearly!

Romans 13:7 Give to everyone what you owe them: If you owe them taxes, pay taxes; if revenue, then revenue; if respect, then respect; if honor, then honor.

He couldn't see anything.

He had fallen into a pit. A pit that was unseen and now he felt so alone and helpless. It was so dark he couldn't even see his hand in front of him. He had been yelling for help and was about to give up when he saw the light shining down upon him. His help had arrived!!

Proverbs 28:13 Whoever conceals their sins does not prosper, but the one who confesses and renounces them finds mercy.

Precious Father, thank You for always keeping Your eyes upon us. We ask You Lord to shine Your light of truth upon our ways. Speak to us, this day, what is unacceptable in Your sight that we are doing in our lives. Place Your finger upon that area that needs to be changed and repentance needs to be asked for. We love You and we praise You in Jesus' name amen.

The Estate owner had the table set.

It was a stunning masterpiece in itself with the elegant tablecloth and the one of a kind fine china with the candelabras and the exquisite flowers.

The food was extraordinary and the best wine money could buy. He was proud to serve his servant who had given of himself.

When it was time for the meal to be served the owner called for him to eat. The servant walked in and was amazed at what he saw before his eyes. Then the servant spoke to his master and said "this isn't for me. I will just sit over to the side and we can still eat together." In the corner stood a small table that hadn't been set for a meal. The owner spoke to him stating all that had been asked of the servant the servant did so and more. The servant explained that he should have done more and that many times he messed up the task that was set before him. He felt unworthy of such honor.

Deuteronomy 7:8 But it was because the Lord loved you and kept the oath He swore to your ancestors that He brought you out with a mighty hand and redeemed you from the land of slavery, from the power of Pharaoh king of Egypt.

Father, thank You for calling us Redeemed and putting a bounty before us. Help us to see ourselves and others as You see. We thank You in Jesus' name amen.

It was a daily occurrence with her.

She kept going back to the "what-ifs" and "if only." She kept thinking of how her life could have been different. Yet, she wasn't embracing the gift of today.

Philippians 3:13 Brothers and sisters, I do not consider myself yet to have taken hold of it. But one thing I do: Forgetting what is behind and straining toward what is ahead.

Father, how we look at our situations and wish things were different. Yes, even wish at times we could go back and change things but God, if it weren't for You things surely could be worse than what they are or were! We thank You for Your goodness and mercy! We give You praise in Jesus' name amen.

He built his "baby" from the ground up.

It was his pride and joy. Nobody could fire him from this position. As a matter of fact, it was he that would do the firing. He was married to his job, his prestige, his reputation and yes, he had a wife. She was the dotting wife all looked at with great pity and even with harsh judgmental eyes.

She stayed by him even through it all. She chose to in spite of all the extramarital affairs, the long hours and the excessive alcohol. All because she saw him for whom he truly was.

She looked at him through the eyes of God. Most thought she stayed with him because of the security in the bank account but it was the security in knowing who she was and Who's she truly belonged to. She didn't battle the "what was fair" but looked to her Redeemer and saw the "bigger picture."

She showed him the love of the Father, the forgiveness of the Father through it all.

John 15:13 "Greater love has no one than this; to lay down one's life for one's friends."

.

Precious Father, You have shown what we are to do. We have lost sight Lord and have gotten caught up in our selfish rights. Forgive us and show us what cup we should bear for another all for Your glory in Jesus' name amen.

She was frantic. How did this happen?

She knew she had to stay calm and listen intently. He couldn't have wandered too far. She knew she had to keep her thoughts focused and not think of the "what if's" and keep looking.

Then she heard them, the cries she knew so well. Yes, she heard the cries of her toddler yelling her name "mommy, mommy where are you?" She ran to him with open arms, cradling his sweet little head.

Psalm 66:19-20 but God has surely listened and has heard my prayer. Praise be to God, Who has not rejected my prayer or withheld His love from me!

Precious Father, thank You for loving us and listening to our hurts, our cries and our desires. Thank You for your outstretched arms that cradle us. We love You in Jesus' name amen.

He kept staring at them, looking at them in every angle he could.

Finally, his dad asked his 6 year old son what he was doing.

The young boy replied "well daddy, your hands are soft when you play trucks with me, when you tickle me and when you push me on the swings. They're soft when you tuck me in bed and when you pick me up and put me on your shoulders. Daddy, they're not so soft when I rub on them though. They have rough places on them but even when you spank me daddy, I don't feel those rough places and I just don't understand that."

The father looking down now at his own hands replied "well my son, what you are actually feeling is my love for you in my hands even when I have to spank you. You see son, these hands are the extension of my love for you."

Job 5:17 Blessed is the one whom God corrects; so do not despise the discipline of the Almighty.

Father, we thank You for chastising us when we error. Forgive us when we have had the wrong mindset going through Your rebuke. We realize it is because You love us and are our good daddy! Thank You in Jesus' name amen.

He was titled a hateful old man. He never smiled nor even so much as extended a wave to those around him.

Nobody would even attempt to get to know him but was willing to believe what they had been told of him.

He had a rough life even from the beginning. He had an alcoholic father who would beat him and his mother and then eventually walked out on them never looking back. He wasn't the quickest learner academically and that caused him even more grief. Later on in his high school years he finally met a young lady who took the time to know who he really was but yet cancer took her from him dashing their dreams of marrying once they graduated. After high school he enlisted in the army to see nothing but brutal deaths and even more heartaches. While overseas he learned of his mothers passing, the only one that understood him, yet he didn't get to say his goodbyes.

Life was pretty hard on his emotions and because of it he withdrew and held onto the bitterness that took root. He needed a friend that would stick closer than anyone had ever done in his life; someone that would listen and learn of who he really was. One that would show him he mattered in this world. At the ripe age of 72 he had a new family move in next door and they had a very energetic 12 year old. This young boy wouldn't allow even those negative words of others sway him from getting to know this old man.

Within months the old man would look forward to his young friend's visits. He felt connected to his young friend even though decade's separated their age. Within time, the young boy started speaking of his other friend named Jesus. He spoke of him so intimately that the old man just had to meet him. He told his little neighbor he could bring him over because he wanted to meet him and that's when his 12 year old friend told him he was in his heart. He led his mature neighbor to the saving knowledge of Jesus Christ and people started seeing the change in the old man. They wanted to know what had brought about his change. Within months the old man had many more friends and felt love like he never had before. He wasn't hard hearted nor closed off to people. As a matter of fact, he felt he had a new heart. He just needed love!

Proverbs 15:13 A glad heart makes a cheerful countenance, but by sorrow of heart the spirit is broken.

Father, forgive us for not looking deeper within the people around us. Forgive us for looking with our mind and not with our souls. How many people, Father, have you placed in our paths to make a difference, yet we looked on the surface of them and criticized their ways? Forgive us Lord and sensitize us to Your heart in Jesus' name amen.

She was such a peaceful woman who many adored.

She had a grace about her, even in her walk. She was beautiful but even more so within. Never would a person hear her complain or belittle someone else. No, as a matter of fact, they would hear her build up those whom others were criticizing. It was as though she knew the most intimate details of all around her. She had led a life that screamed for redemption and she knew when she received it just how blessed she was. No one in the world could ever forgive her the way her Jesus had. She didn't take her sins being wiped away lightly. It's because of this mindset she was able to see others around her with different eyes. Yes, she saw them with spiritual eyes and not in the natural. This is what gave her the air of grace she walked in.

She knew redemption and knew that is what everyone needed. She knew much had been forgiven in her life and she wasn't going to condemn those who were doing what she had done.

Romans 4:7-8 'Blessed are those whose transgressions are forgiven, whose sins are covered. Blessed is the one whose sin the Lord will never count against them.'

Father, forgive us for being critical of those who are doing what we have been forgiven of. Forgive us of our nasty attitudes of being totally unappreciative of what You have done for us. We thank You God for wiping away our sins, in Jesus' name amen.

Word of the Lord:

"My precious people watch out for your flesh wants to rule and side with your "temporal mind". Beware of the tricks of the adversary for his season, right now, is to start pulling on My very elect and to persuade them. Stand firm, stand ground and see the salvation of My hand! Yes," says the Lord, "he has his seasons of play as well. Draw unto Me and he won't take you off guard for I will show you how to fight and how to stand! This is a time for My children to hide themselves under My wings and to dig into My word even more so. It will be a season of great revelation of what I have been speaking. Watch your hearts and do not let them be cold. Pray even more so for those who are coming against you. Remember, it is actually Me they are coming against! Remain in Me in the ways I direct, for others will have other game plans I have set for them. Do not look to the left nor look to the right but keep your eyes fixed on THE GREAT I AM!! For I AM is your salvation" says the Lord!

He was spoken of often.

He was a person of interest in many circles of society. Many times he was looked at as one who was a little bizarre. He was also looked at as one of unspeakable love; a love like no other.

Numerous time people would find that their meals had been paid for, bills paid in full, and other times a handful of cash when they needed it most. People didn't have to ask him, he did it because that was who he was. Most often, they would question why he chose them to be blessed. It wasn't what they did or could do, no; it was their season of need and also their season of blessings. When he passed many grieved but yet they found it appeared he was still alive as blessings of the past still happened. He was still actively blessing peoples' lives as though he was living amongst them.

Psalm 31:19 How abundant are the good things that you have stored up for those who fear you, that you bestow in the sight of all, on those who take refuge in you.

Father, Your blessings are continually before us. Thank You that You bless us and love on us at all times. We call ourselves blessed beyond measure in Jesus' name amen!

He wanted that million dollar view.

He was known around the world for his beautiful architectural homes.

Now it was time for him to build one for himself. This was going to be the best of the best and he wasn't going to leave anything undone.

He wasn't going to have just a million dollar view, no; it was to be a multi-million dollar view. He started to build and when he did people started questioning him about his location. He was annoyed "who do they think I am? I know how to build!"

When he was finished with his breathtaking build with its gorgeous views people would look in awe. But it was at the back of everyone's mind "what was he thinking building it here? He is a master builder, he should know better."

Then it happened. A storm of great magnitude hit and his beautiful home was gone in the blink of an eye. It would not have been so if he would have heeded the advice of those who cared for him. No, he thought he knew all and now his home was no longer.

Proverbs 8:33 Listen to my instruction and be wise; do not disregard it.

Proverbs 16:18 Pride goes before destruction, a haughty spirit before a fall.

Father, forgive us for thinking more highly of ourselves than we should. You put people in our path to help us with this walk of life. Please sensitize us even more so to live our lives to its fullness. Thank You Lord in Jesus' name amen.

They studied the land.

They had to make sure they had a good foundation that they would be building their home upon.

1 Corinthians 3:10 By the grace God has given me, I laid a foundation as a wise builder, and someone else is building on it. But each one should build with care.

Father, You are so amazing!! Thank You for building character in our lives. Please reveal the foundations and if there are cracks or weakened areas we ask You to repair them. Help us to see what stones we have been carrying around and even what we have been building upon. We thank You in Jesus 'name amen!!

They gave to boast in their works.

Then she stood and went forward. She couldn't afford much but what she did give she gave from her heart.

Luke 21:1-4 As Jesus looked up, he saw the rich putting their gifts into the temple treasury. He also saw a poor widow put in two very small copper coins. "Truly I tell you, he said, "this poor widow has put in more than all others. All these people gave their gifts out of their wealth; but she out of her poverty put in all she had to live on."

Father, You ask that we give from our hearts and not out of duty. This isn't just financially but in all that we do. Help us Father to do just that – give of ourselves from the heart just as You did we pray in Jesus' name amen.

He worked hard in obtaining possessions and having a hefty bank account.

He put a lot of trust into his possessions and job thinking that it would bring him happiness and security.

Psalm 11:28 "Those who trust in their riches will fall, but the righteous will thrive like a green leaf.

Precious Father, we come boldly to You with thankful hearts that we can. Lord, Your word says to not trust in anything apart from You. We come humbly asking You to show us if and where we have placed our confidence in. Please Father, reveal to us what we have trusted in more than You in Jesus' name amen!

Word of the Lord:

"My children, have I not told you the enemy has come to kill, to steal and destroy? Have I also not told you that I have come to give you life and life abundantly (John 10:10)? I ask you now, who do you have your hands stretched out to? Is it to the enemy so that he can keep taking, destroying and killing those things that are rightfully yours? Are you going to keep allowing him to kill the dreams I have put within you? Are you going to keep allowing him to steal the hope and joy I have freely given to you? Are you going to allow him to destroy the freedom I purchased for you? My precious children, stop giving in to him and stretch forth your hands and receive what I have been trying to give to you! I AM willing to restore your hands to receive the goodness I have for you" says the Lord! (Mark 3:5) "Freely receive this day My goodness."

Where was He?

She needed Him and yet she couldn't hear Him. She was on her knees crying out. She was praying hard yet she felt her prayers weren't being received. She was doing good deeds thinking they would grab His attention. Then one day she quieted herself and started to wait.

1 Kings 19:11-12 The LORD said, "Go out and stand on the mountain in the presence of the LORD, for the LORD is about to pass by." Then a great and powerful wind tore the mountains apart and shattered the rocks before the LORD, but the LORD was not in the wind. After the wind there was a great earthquake, but the LORD was not in the earthquake. After the earthquake came a fire, but the LORD was not in the fire. And after the fire came a gentle whisper.

Father, help us to listen to Your voice in the loud world around us. May we quiet ourselves to hear Your precious voice in Jesus' name amen.

He was a carpenter by trade yet he had such a gift.

It didn't matter what type of wood or what was needed, he could do a wonder with what he was working on. He could take a piece of wood that was beaten and battered by the elements and make a beautiful masterpiece.

He saw such beauty in the piece of raw wood and saw even more beauty in it after he worked it. He saw the end work in the beginning process. He poured himself in his work until the job was completed.

Father, thank You for seeing who we were made to be! Thank You for giving Your Son for us. Please help us to realize and obtain the love You have poured out to us. You took a rough, cruel piece of wood and poured Your all out for each and every one of us -pure love, a love that is tangible. The cross You bore turned into a masterpiece of beautiful love! We thank You in Jesus' name amen.

He thought on it all the time.

He was now in his late 60's and enjoying life, grand babies and growing old with his wife. Yet, it was always on his mind and he said he forgave.

The memories of his highschool prom were as if it happened yesterday. The beauty of his sweetheart, now wife, the laughter of their friends, the music as if it were still playing and then also, the fight between what was his best friend and another young man. The fight became physical and then deadly. No one saw it coming until it was too late. The other man withdrew a knife and stabbed his friend in the heart. Immediately, they all knew he was dead.

Years have obviously past and yet he gets angry with his best friends assaulter. The 'what if's and could have been's" plague his mind. Then one day he heard his Heavenly Father's voice question him "when will you forgive?" Immediately, he replies "I already have" to hear the confronting words of "no son, you have not. True forgiveness is what I have done for you. I do not sit and replay your shortcomings and sins and get upset or angry. No, I have thrown them away as far away as the East is from the West. That's true forgiveness!"

Psalm 103:12 as far as the East is from the West, so far has he removed our transgressions from us.

Father, forgive us for just saying 'we forgive' in words and not in spirit. Convict us this day, Lord, in what we are still holding on to. We thank You, Father, for the forgiveness You have given us time after time! We pray this in Jesus' name amen!

He couldn't take his eyes off her.

Wherever she was, he would fix his eyes to her. Yes, many times he would hear of her "less than desirable" lifestyle, especially a man of his rank in society. Yet, he simply did not care. Many times he would tell her accusers to quiet their talk. He saw far more greatness in her than what the people ever could. She had his complete attention no matter what was told to him or shown to him. She was the center of his attention and nothing could change it. How many times others would say to him "she will never change, just watch, she is bound to keep repeating her 'sins'." All the while, he kept saying "she hasn't found true love like I have for her. She is beautiful inside as well, I know it."

Ephesians 3:19 and to know this love that surpasses knowledge – that you may be filled to the measure of all the fullness of God

Precious Father, Your amazing love is so pure, so undefiled, that it seems so foreign in this crazy world. We thank You for Your forgiveness, for Your attention you give us. This day, Father, make it even more real than before. In Jesus' name amen!

She didn't think she could do it any longer.

Her mom was in failing health, her husband was not the attentive man she was longing for, her child was in a world of rebellion and her work was threatening to shut its doors. How could she put her foot in front of the other when she couldn't even focus on even the simplest of tasks?

Thank goodness breathing was an automatic. Her world was, without a doubt, spinning out of control and she was hanging on by a thread. Then she heard His still, quiet voice speaking ever so passionately to her, "My precious child, I see you struggling and I say peace to your storm." It was in that moment that she realized not once had she stopped to even breath a prayer of help, a prayer for grace to look at those around her that were struggling in their own issues of life. She dropped to her knees and bowed her head in reverence to THE KEEPER of her soul and cried for repentance. She allowed the trials of life to escape from her into her Savior's hands.

Psalm 29:11 "The Lord gives strength to his people; the Lord blesses His people with peace."

Father, precious Father, the trials in life seem to be overbearing please speak into our spirit at this moment. Please forgive us for trying in our own strength. We love You in Jesus' name amen!

Refreshed, revived, and so brand new.

She remembers as if it were yesterday. She was standing in front of the mirror looking at eyes that were dead and hollow. She had no life, no zeal or hope in them or inside of her. She was a walking corpse.

All of life's decisions and her actions had led her down a road of much confusion, resentment and hatred towards herself. She was so disgusted with how life was turning out and there seemed to be no end to the mess called her life.

Where did it all start and would it ever end?

She calls her "her angel" and she will always be so very grateful for her. She knew her from nowhere and yet she had what she wanted. She had the zeal, the joy and the love she was looking for. Her "angel" knew she was in dire straits and took her to a place of love. She took the time to teach her about a love so pure, so real and so needed. She told her about THE Father's love.

Since that time, she has come to experience His love first hand and now shares it with others. Now she looks at a new person in the mirror and loves the person she sees. She sees the Father's love through her eyes and in her actions. She is a new person, as the old has passed away!

2 Corinthians 5:17 "Therefore, if anyone is in Christ, the new creation has come: The old has gone, the new is here!"

Father, thank You for the new person You have made us to be. Help us Father not to look back at the old person as that person is no longer alive. We thank You for Who You are and we love You, in Jesus' name amen!

It was a relationship most would run from.

He loved her with all he had in him and yet she wasn't a faithful partner. "How can you possibly stay with her?" was the popular question. His simple and yet so profound statement "because I love her" would leave them scratching their heads.

His love was an everlasting love and no matter what she did or didn't do, it would not affect his love for her. More times than not, she, herself, couldn't understand him and his unending love.

The book of Hosea is a perfect portrayal of the love of our Heavenly Father has for us, the harlot, in which we are ever so much committing adultery against Him. Yet, His love is continually for us. His love is perfect love!

Hosea 3:1 "The Lord said to me, Go, show our love to your wife again, though she is loved by another man and is an adulteress. Love her as the Lord loves the Israelites, though they turn to other gods and love the sacred raisin cakes."

Father, how can You keep staying with us, the unfaithful? Nevertheless, we thank You and we keep asking for Your forgiveness. We thank You for Who You are and we praise You! In Jesus' name amen!!

He grabbed a handful of dirt.

In it He saw beauty and inspiration.

So too often, we cast aside His ability or even His desire to work with what we are going through. We mutter through our tears of frustration, that we have really done a number and then we carry around condemnation and we wear it as jewelry around our necks. It stifles us and chokes out the breath within us.

In Isaiah 64:8 it speaks of us being the clay while our Father is the Potter. Since this is so, why not hop up on the Potter's wheel and watch Him work out the troubles in our lives? His hands are ever so gentle. He won't hurt us while He is working on us! Let Him massage out the kinks in our situations.

Isaiah 64:8 "Yet you, Lord, are our Father. We are the clay, you are the potter; we are all the work of your hand."

Precious Father, we come with our hands held out to You with all things troubling us. Please take these things and us and work them out all for Your glory. Thank You, Father, for making our dirt good in Jesus' name amen!

He was diving into The Word, his praise was continual, and his prayers were soaring to heaven. He was meditating on God day and night. Then it came!

How sneaky it was, so subtle, and yet so very powerful. "It" was the spirit of offense. Instead of repenting and releasing he held on to it and it grew. It grew from offense to resentment to bitterness to hate and then murder in his heart.

No longer were the praises coming. No longer the meditations or prayers that seemed to have wings. Instead it was as though belittling words, complaints and prayers of iron.

How did this happen? Be careful in what you let come in and take charge because it will control you!

Song of Solomon 2:15 "Catch for us the foxes, the little foxes that ruin the vineyards, our vineyards that are in bloom."

Proverbs 4:23 "Above all else, guard your heart, for everything you do flows from it."

Father, help us keep our hearts tuned into you. Help us not to let the little things in life overwhelm us and then control us. Let us be controlled by Holy Spirit. Prick our conscience when we start to become off balanced in Jesus' name amen!

He felt like he was spinning his wheels.

He felt that he kept getting knocked down for doing what was right and those who were doing wrong were advancing.

He knew he had to keep going. He knew doing right was the only way to go.

2 Thessalonians 3:13 "And as for you, brothers and sisters, never tire of doing what is good."

Father, forgive us for looking at the worlds standards and not keeping our focus on You. It's You who will reward us far better than this old world. Help us keep our focus on Who really matters, You! We love You, in Jesus' name amen!

She picked up the figurine.

Looking it over and then placing it back on the shelf she took inventory.

So many knick-knacks were all about in her house. Many hours she worked just to obtain another item. She thought it would bring her happiness but ultimately in the end it brought only a moments pleasure.

Habakkuk 2:18 "Of what value is an idol carved by a craftsman? Or an image that teaches lies? For the one who makes it trusts in his own creation; he makes idols that cannot speak."

Father, we come asking that You show us what we have made idols of.

Forgive us for trading in Your everlasting love for items that are to be consumed by fire. In Jesus' name amen.

How was she to accomplish this task?

She felt all alone in it. It was bigger than her and she felt inadequate.

She knew she heard the Lords calling and she knew she just had to trust.

Psalm 32:8 "I will instruct you and teach you in the way you should go; I will counsel you with my loving eye on you."

Father, thank You for Your trust in us to do what You have called us to do. Thank You for Your leading. Thank You that Your Word says You will direct us and help us to remember Your promise as we step out and proceed with what You have called us to. In Jesus' name amen.

His aim was off.

He was a skilled marksman and had the medals to show but lately he couldn't accurately hit his mark. He knew he had to regroup and concentrate on what was before him.

In this life you will sin or as the meaning of sin states "miss the mark." You will inevitably do something that goes against our Heavenly Father. We are not without sin and when this happens we need to realize we need to repent and ask God to help us learn from it and move on.

When Christ died on the cross for our sins His blood that he shed is now our covering. When we repent and turn away from our wrongs God sees the blood of His Son over each and every one of us that have accepted Christ as Lord.

1 Peter 2:24 "He himself bore our sins" in his body on the cross, so that we might die to sins and live for righteousness; "by his wounds you have been healed."

Psalm 37:24 "though he may stumble, he will not fall, for the Lord upholds him with his hand."

Father, thank You for Your love and forgiveness. Help us to walk in it all for Your glory. Thank You that You have us in the precious name of Jesus amen!

She kept rubbing her eyes.

Taking her glasses on and off she just could not see clearly.

What is it that you are blinded from? Is it the love of the Father? Is it the fact that you need a Saviour? Whatever it may be, ask God for new spiritual eyesight. He is so very willing!

John 9:6-7 "After saying this, he spat on the ground made some mud with the saliva, and put it on the man's eyes. "Go," he told him, "wash in the Pool of Siloam" (this word means "Sent"). So the man went and washed, and came home seeing."

Father, this world can blind us with its ways. Even man's ways blinds us from seeing You. Father, we come asking now, right now, for Your ointment. We ask for new spiritual eyes to see You and Your ways and love! Father, it's all about You! We pray in the most precious name Jesus!!

He knew he was where he was to be.

So many people were trying to persuade him to give up. Yet, he knew he was to have this blessing.

Romans 4:21 "being fully persuaded that God had power to do what he had promised."

Father, forgive us for giving in so easily to the pressures around us. Forgive us for not seeing the blessings You have bestowed to us. Show us, this day, our blessings that You, Lord, have graciously given. Help us to stand our ground and let nothing come between You and our blessings. We thank You in Jesus' name amen!

He became accustomed to his situation.

He accepted that nothing in his life was going to change and allowed himself to settle for how it was; he resigned that this was his life.

John 5:6-7 "When Jesus saw him lying there and learned that he had been in this condition for a long time, he asked him, "Do you want to get well?" "Sir," the invalid replied, "I have no one to help me into the pool when the water is stirred. While I am trying to get in, someone else goes down ahead of me.""

Father God, we come to You with a repentant heart and apologize for embracing the issues around us instead of embracing You. Show us what mindsets we have. Help us to not use excuses and to advance in You. In Jesus' name amen.

Did it really matter that he had all these materialistic things?

What he considered to be of worth would anyone else once he was gone? Everything he strived for was something that could be destroyed in a matter of minutes. What he would give to take back the time that he spent storing up. He should have been toiling in the spirit for the generations behind him.

King Solomon wrote in Ecclesiastes 2:10-11 "I denied myself nothing my eyes desired; I refused my heart no pleasure. My heart took delight in all my labor, and this was the reward for all my toil. Yet when I surveyed all that my hands had done and what I had toiled to achieve, everything was meaningless, a chasing after the wind; nothing was gained under the sun"

Father, make it be known what we are leaving behind for this generation and for those after. Help us to see what we are truly striving for. Forgive us for being senseless with our time in Jesus' name amen!

They stretched forth their hands and shook on it.

Although many said they should have drawn up a contract, they took each other at their word.

Matthew 8:8 "the centurion replied, "Lord, I do not deserve to have you come under my roof. But just say the word, and my servant will be healed."

My question to you is do you take Him at His word? Has God spoken something to you and is He waiting on you to take Him at His word? He has done His part, have you done yours?

Father, we know You are not man that You can lie. We ask forgiveness now for being unfaithful to Your words. We ask now Father to knock down those walls that hinder us in taking You at Your word. In Jesus' name amen.

She knew she had to let it go.

Rehearsing it over and over in her head was only causing her more grief; not just physically but spiritually as well. Mulling it over was only holding her prisoner.

Exodus 7:14 "then the LORD said to Moses, "Pharaoh's heart is unyielding; he refuses to let the people go."

Heavenly Father, it's a trial to let some issues go. Help us not to be a prisoner in our own minds and hearts. Please take these emotions and heal our hurts. We release these hurts to You. We trust You Abba Father! In Jesus' name amen.

She was on top of the world.

Then life hit and she felt she was at the bottom of the barrel. Why was it that she seemed to only draw on God when things were in turmoil?

Exodus 8:15 "But when Pharaoh saw that there was relief, he hardened his heart and would not listen to Moses and Aaron, just as the Lord had said."

Father, how many times do we ignore You when all seems well in our world? Forgive us when we only think upon You when we are in despair. We thank You for Your grace and we repent with all of our hearts in Jesus' name amen.

She pulled out the yellowed piece of paper.

She could quote it without having to read it. She remembered the words word for word. She held onto the words God had spoken to her knowing that in due time they would surely come to pass.

Luke 2:19 "But Mary treasured up all these things and pondered them in her heart."

Father God, those things in which You have spoken to us we ask You to help us hold on to them. Help us know that in the proper season we will see them manifest. For those words that we have put from us help us to draw them back out and blow the dust off of them. Thank You that You are a perfect and loving daddy. We pray this in Jesus' name amen.

He had it all but all was not enough.

Unfortunately he would find out the hard way.

Yes, he had a good life in the eyes of society and yet he felt he needed to go out and see how much more was out there. He lived to party and flash his money around until it was all gone. He then hit bottom realizing just where he came from. He knew he had better and that this way of living wasn't meant for him. He had to return to his father and his fathers love even if it meant being made a servant. He knew where to come back to.

How many of us have pulled away from God believing the world had more to give to just find out we were more empty than ever? No matter what we have done, God is a good daddy waiting for us. Don't let the past dealings keep you in the pig pen, come back home. Get your hearts condition straightened out by Abba Father. He has the best of parties to throw for you!

Luke 15:20 So he got up and went to his father. "But while he was still a long way off, his father saw him and was filled with compassion for him; he ran to his son, threw his arms around him and kissed him.

Father, thank You for looking after us, waiting for us to return unto You. Thank You for never throwing our sins up in our face. Thank You for taking us back as Your true sons and daughters. We love You in Jesus' name amen.

Tick tock went the clock.

He viewed time as his enemy. He didn't see himself being able to complete the task now that he was much older.

Genesis 17:17 Abraham fell facedown; he laughed and said to himself, "Will a son be born to a man a hundred years old? Will Sarah bear a child at the age of ninety?"

How many of us have thought we have missed it? Missed our calling because we think we might have fallen short one too many times or because of our age or because we simply just think we aren't capable? Have you laughed at God as Abraham did in verse 17? If so, do you not know it is God Who is the One that will carry you forth in what He has called you to do? Reach for the blessings He has put in front of you and answer the call!

Heavenly Father, we ask for forgiveness for denying what You have called us to do. We ask Lord for a fresh wind in You! Forgive us for looking at the natural and thank You for not giving up on us in Jesus' name amen.

She chose not to think upon the negatives in her life.

Instead she would allow the loving and peaceful memories to drive her.

What is it that you are giving your attention to? Where is it that you are putting your mind to? Are you concentrating on the yuck of this world or are you thinking on the glory of God?

Philippians 4:8 Finally, brothers and sisters, whatever is true, whatever is noble, whatever is right, whatever is lovely, whatever is admirable-if anything is excellent or praiseworthy-think about such things.

Give God the glory He is so due and watch where you put your mind on.

Father, forgive us for wasting our time on focusing on the negatives instead of seeing the beautiful blessings You have put in front of us. Sensitize our minds Lord to see You in which You are all around us in Jesus' name amen!

He had such a giving spirit.

He didn't have issues with giving to those who were in need. In all honesty, he delighted in giving to others.

Ruth 2:15-16 As she got up to glean, Boaz gave orders to his men, "Let her gather among the sheaves and don't reprimand her. Even pull out some stalks for her from the bundles and leave them for her to pick up, and don't rebuke her."

Father, help us to leave nuggets behind for those who are in need. Help us Lord, to show the love of You to those around us. You have blessed us to be a blessing. In Jesus' name amen.

She had her bags packed.

She knew nothing of where she was going or of the people. She just had the love in her heart to follow the one she loved.

Ruth 1:16-17 But Ruth replied, "Don't urge me to leave you or to turn back from you. Where you go I will go, and where you stay I will stay. Your people will be my people and your God my God. Where you die I will die, and there I will be buried. May the Lord deal with me, be it ever so severely, if even death separates you and me."

Father, You have a plan for us. Help us to leave our desires behind to follow the path You have set before us. Let us say "Your ways and not ours." In Jesus' name amen.

Word of the Lord:

The Lord says "My people need to move forward and advance in Me. Many things, many great blessings are waiting for them but progress needs to be achieved. Know this, I AM is here and waiting. Will you trust Me to bring you forward?"

I was awake very early this morning and God gave me a vision with some heavy words.

The vision was a dirt road that had mature, green trees on both sides of this road. The road was very peaceful and serene. Then He spoke "My people curse their roads to their blessings and breakthroughs."

When Paul was asking God to remove the thorn from his side God spoke "My grace is sufficient." The pain was needed for Paul. You can read in Job that through his horrendous ordeals God asked him if he was the one who called things in order. Again, it was needed for Job to go through his troubling times.

It all brings us to the point that it is God and God alone who is sovereign and He knows what needs to happen in our lives to bring about His promotion for our lives.

Too many are eager to point the finger of Satan attacking us but he cannot without God's approval! Pain shows us we are alive and very aware of our flesh. The pain or trials shows us who is actually in charge of our being.

Notice whatever your trial is what it brings out of you. Does it bring about a nasty attitude or does it bring out the thought of just giving up? Does it bring about you on your knees? Does it bring out of you more of a hunger to dive into His word and to praise Him?

The path (dirt road) that is before us is lined by His hand and He has us covered. Are you cursing your road or are you saying as Paul did that you count it a blessing because God sees that you are worthy to go through the trials?

He is a good and awesome daddy who has nothing but the very best for His children!

Abba Father, we come asking for forgiveness for wanting the easy way out. For not reflecting that it is You who knows best. Father, help us through these times to rely on You and Your grace and not mere man or our shallow thinking. We love You daddy in Jesus' name amen.

Why?

Why was it that he saw others being continually blessed? He wasn't looking at all the blessings that had been bestowed upon him. Instead he allowed jealousy to take control.

Genesis 37:4 When his brothers saw that their father loved him more than an of them, they hated him and could not speak a kind word to him.

Precious Father, let this be the year where we stand before You and see what truly is within us. Let this be the year we truly become united as siblings in Your household. Forgive us, Father, for coming against Your family! Help us see the love that You have poured out for all of us and that You are not a respecter of persons. Show us the numerous blessings that is upon our own lives and not to look at our neighbors with envy. In Jesus' name amen.

Couldn't they see she was busy?

So much work and yet no body was helping her. Instead they were listening to him.

Luke 10:38-42 As Jesus and his disciples were on their way, he came to a village where a woman named Martha opened her home to him. She had a sister called Mary, who sat at the Lord's feet listening to what he said. But Martha was distracted by all the preparations that had to be made. She came to him and asked, "Lord, don't you care that my sister has left me to do the work by myself? Tell her to help me!" "Martha, Martha," the Lord answered, "you are worried and upset about many things, but few things are needed-or indeed only one. Mary has chosen what is better, and it will not be taken away from her."

Father, we come now repenting of allowing other things to take place over You. Forgive us for not taking the much needed time to spend at Your feet. At Your feet is where we find the refreshing our souls need. Thank You for Your forgiveness in Jesus' name amen.

She was all over the road.

Instead of her looking ahead she kept looking in her rearview mirror.

Genesis 19:26 But Lot's wife looked back, and she became a pillar of salt.

Father God, in all Your love and wisdom we ask that You show us what we are allowing to keep us from pushing ahead, what it is that we keep looking back on. Father, we choose to go forward with Your grace in this season and we thank You for Your healing virtue in Christ Jesus' name amen!

How could she keep going?

Day after day it was a battle. If it weren't issues at her job they were there at home. Adversities seemed to be before her and behind her. No matter which way she turned she was struggling. What was she to do?

Isaiah 30:20-21 Although the Lord gives you the bread of adversity and the water of affliction, your teachers will be hidden no more; with your own eyes you will see them. Whether you turn to the right or to the left, your ears will hear a voice behind you, saying, "This is the way; walk in it."

Father, there seems to be seasons where it's a chore to put one foot in front of the other due to all the struggles we face. Help us to see that there is a plan in it all and that You have us. You will teach us what we are to glean from these trials. Help us Father, to see You in them all. In Jesus' name amen.

The word of the Lord:

"You who say you know Me, do you really? Do you know that I shower you with My love? Do you know that My face shines upon you? Do you know I count you worthy? Do you know I delight in you? Do you My children? Do you? Then why is it that your head is hung low? Why is it you run from Me instead of run to Me when you find yourself in distress? Come unto Me and watch how I pour Myself out to you! No, My children I do not hold you afar but I hold you in the palm of My hand. I AM here for you, yes, come unto Me My beloved! Come unto Me with your head held high because you find yourself in Me" says the Lord.

He had traveled this path before.

Then it was a bit harder. Now he knew where to turn and where not to go. This road was now being walked with his friend.

Proverbs 27:17 As iron sharpens iron, so one person sharpens another.

Father, we go through issues not just for ourselves but also for one another. Sometimes these roads we travel in life are to help those who will too walk them. Help us to extend our hand to those in their time of need. Help us to encourage one another in Jesus' name amen.

Word of the Lord:

"Do not think, says the Lord, that anything that is done unto Me is not rewarded! No, says the Lord, for I AM a good daddy that loves to reward My children. Work unto Me and watch Me shower My blessings upon you. Do not look for mans reward as it is a vapor and will be forgotten, but work unto your Father, who forgets not!"

His imagination was going wild.

He could hear the praises of his peers. He wanted to hear just how great his actions were and receive their attention.

Matthew 6:1 "Be careful not to practice your righteousness in front of others to be seen by them. If you do, you will have no reward from your Father in heaven."

Father God, we come now Lord asking for forgiveness in all things that we have done for mans kind words and not unto You. Father God, we ask You now to prick our hearts when we set out to do things for mans approval. Check our hearts Lord, show us this day, where we need to change. We pray this all for Your glory in Jesus' name amen.

She knew where to look.

It was a tree in her neighbors' yard. Anytime life was getting hard she would stare at that particular tree and see what it had battled. Some limbs were missing and the bark was falling off in places yet it was leaning. It was leaning toward the heavens.

Isaiah 26:3-4 You will keep in perfect peace those whose minds are steadfast, because they trust in you. Trust in the Lord forever, for the Lord, the Lord himself, is the Rock eternal.

Father, we will continually stand when we lean on You. You are our strength and our help. No matter the battles and the scars we receive, if we continually lean on You we will make it. Thank You in Jesus' name amen.

Word of the Lord:

"Yes," says the Spirit of the Lord, "I have been very gracious with you but no flesh will glory in My presence. I will strip away all fleshly motives and ideas and will reveal the true hearts of men. This is a year of renewed faith, a newness of love for Me says the Lord. This is going to be a time of great understanding of who I truly AM! I AM putting a fresh zeal for Me in My people and they are going to know that the yoke has been broken off of their necks. Yes, they are going to breath in Me and not mere man. This newness in Me will reveal great giftings that I have put within My people. New ideas and inventions will come forth from the bonds of men being broken. My people will have a fresh breath, a fresh wind of revelation for Me that will come only from Me for Me says the Lord! Be ye doers of My word, yes, but for the right reasons – for My glory and no other. If My people are willing, this will be the year for My people for My glory."

The atmosphere was charged with such joy and excitement.

As they sat the cake, all aglow with 82 candles in front of her, she saw her young life playing in slow motion through her mind. Yes, God had held her hand through many times of trials and tremendous times of joy.

Lamentations 3:21-23 Because of the Lord's great love we are not consumed, for his compassions never fail. They are new every morning; great is your faithfulness.

Father, You hold us in Your hand. You, Father, shower us with Your mercies and faithfulness and because of this we know we have the abilities to go forth in our day that You've set before us. Thank You for Your love, mercies and faithfulness everyday in Jesus' name amen.

Word of the Lord:

For the Spirit of the LORD says "My people, hear My voice! Hear what I have to speak to you – come, come to Me and listen to what I have to say to you. Find yourself saturated in My love. Find yourself lost in My presence. In this place you will find yourself and those things that consume you fall off. Come to Me with all that has you bound for I say," says the LORD, "no more – let the chains fall!"

If anything could come against him it was.

He was normally an easy going guy but now he was noticing his temper was quick and his peaceful spirit was anything but peaceful. Where did things start to turn? It was the reports he was receiving that he was viewing as negative. It was the lack of prayer and neglecting reading God's word that was taking away his peace. Yes, it was these small foxes that were spoiling the vine of his peace.

Song of Solomon 2:15 Catch for us the foxes, the little foxes that run the vineyards, our vineyards that are in bloom.

Father, how we allow the enemy and our minds to take us from Your presence. Forgive us for leaving Your peace and joy. Show us Father, where we have let the small foxes spoil our vines and help us trap them with Your word in Jesus' name amen!

"What is wrong with this silly thing?" she questioned.

She had checked numerous times that it was plugged in and every time she saw that it was. She kept hitting the switch but to no avail then she saw the issue. Although the plug was plugged into the extension cord, the extension cord wasn't plugged in.

John 15:5 "I am the vine; you are the branches. If you remain in me and I in you, you will bear much fruit; apart from me you can do nothing."

Father, how we get so entangled with worldly duties that we forsake our private times with You. Forgive us ABBA Father, as nothing can compare to our "Daddy time." We love You in Jesus' name amen!

How could they have been broken into?

After all, they had the state of the art security system. Then the realization hit them, they forgot to turn it on!

So often in our Christian walk we turn off our "security system" in that we ignore either the promptings of Holy Spirit or the convictions of Holy Spirit. Unfortunately, we at times do both.

Romans 8:6 The mind governed by the flesh is death, but the mind governed by the Spirit is life and peace

Father, we repent for ignoring You and ask that we become even more in tune to Your promptings and warnings. Forgive us for leaning into our own understandings in Jesus' name amen!

The bars were cold as ice as she gripped them tightly.

She knew there was fresh air to be breathed and warmth from the sun to be felt yet she was holding on to the cold bars she had grown to know. She was again holding on to the bars of imprisonment of her heart and mind.

She didn't want to give in to the truth that she could be set free. Set free from the pain of past actions, whether she did them or they were done to her. No, she didn't want the chance of failure or the chance of being hurt again to happen. She was refusing the freedom that had been freely given to her.

John 8:36 So if the Son sets you free, you will be free indeed.

Precious Father, thank You for setting us free from our past mistakes. Thank You for showing us what true forgiveness is. Forgive us now Father, for holding ourselves prisoners in our sins and not forgiving those whom we need to. In Jesus' name amen.

It was a daily occurrence with her.

She kept going back to the "what-ifs" and "if onlys." She kept thinking of how her life could have been different. Yet, she wasn't embracing the gift of today.

In Luke it talks of those who keep looking back isn't of any use to the Kingdom. We need to stop beating ourselves up over past mistakes and look forward to the grace God has extended to us daily.

Luke 9:62 Jesus replied, "No one who puts a hand to the plow and looks back is fit for service in the kingdom of God."

Who said what you deem as a mistake God hasn't used to get you to where you are now? All too often we look with dimly lit eyes at not just our past but even our present and future. We are held in the palm of our Heavenly Fathers hand.

Choose this day to walk in praises of His grace!

Father, how we look at our situations and wish things were different. Yes, even wish at times we could go back and change things but God, if it weren't for You things surely could be worse than what they are or were! We thank You for Your goodness and mercy! We give You praise in Jesus' name amen.

They were the best of friends.

All five of them connected immediately when they first met in college. They were brothers from the heart.

They had each others back and stood tall for the others. They were all there when they married. They lived within miles of one another and all had very lucrative jobs. Their wives were just as close to each other as well. Yes, they were family. No one took a vacation without the others. Expensive cars, clothes, jewelry, homes, you name it they all kept up with the other.

Then it hit! No longer could one couple continue with the outlandish lifestyle, yet how could they pull back? The husband and wife knew it would be a blow to their pride but they were now swimming in a sea of unrelenting debt; debt that was taking them down fast. They had to break from the vacations and outings and doing so would mean becoming open with their deepest friends.

The meeting came with their friends and out came their secret of extreme debt and no longer being able to carry their previous lifestyle. What came from them being forth coming shocked them; one by one the couples admitted they could not continue with what had become the norm.

It was life changing and from that couple being real with the others set the ball in motion of becoming free from their burdens.

What we don't realize is we have people watching our lives. They are checking whether our walk with Christ is real. Can we simply state to them "it's going to be alright" or can we be real with them and say "I too am struggling with this issue"? All too often we think we have to hide but the ball is waiting to be put in motion.

Proverbs 11:2 When pride comes, them comes disgrace, but with humility comes wisdom.

Father God, we come now asking forgiveness for our prideful ways. How many people have you put before us to help break free or to be freed from something but hid? Show us Father what we need to do to put things in motion in Jesus' name amen

He would not let anybody in his life.

He had been wounded numerous times and the hurts were unbearable.

Genesis 29:3 When all the flocks were gathered there, the shepherds would roll the stone away from the well's mouth and water the sheep. Then they would return the stone to its place over the mouth of the well.

For obvious reasons there was a stone rolled on top of the well to prevent animals and people from falling in and other issues of the sort. But also with this stone on top it would not allow anything to be drawn from it; nothing could come up and out from it.

Is there a stone over your well? Do you have fear, denial or lack of trust? What is keeping you or anyone else from drawing from the "Well of Living Waters" that is within you? Do you not know God has put something of great value inside each and every one of us that is refreshing waters to someone in need?

Roll the stone away and allow the waters to be drawn from!

Father God, thank You for the "Well of Living Waters" that You have placed inside of us. Forgive us for rolling a stone on top of it due to our own fears. Show us what our stones are all about so that we can accomplish the tasks You have set before us. We thank You in Jesus' name amen!

She had a tight grip.

Her confidence was wrapped in all her worldly possessions and ideas.

Too often we say we have confidence in God yet we have our arms wrapped around something else.

If you were to ask God what would He tell you your confidence is in? Do you have your confidence in your money, in your job or is it in friends or family? It's a strong question to ask ourselves but yet a very deep question that needs to be revealed. We need to humble ourselves before our LORD and ask Him to show us where our true confidence is found.

Isaiah 28:20 The bed is too short to stretch out on, the blanket too narrow to wrap around you.

This scripture is saying that those things in which you have confidence in cannot help you. They cannot bring us comfort.

Precious Father, we come boldly to You with thankful hearts that we can. We come humbly asking You to show us where and whom we have placed our confidence in. Please Father, reveal to us what we need to know in Jesus' name amen.

Word of the Lord:

My children, have I not told you the enemy has come to kill, to steal and destroy? Have I also not told you that I have come to give you life and life abundantly (John 10:10)? I ask you now who do you have your hands stretched out to? Is it to the enemy so that he can keep taking, destroying and killing those things that are rightfully yours? Are you going to keep allowing him to kill the dreams I have put with in you? Are you going to keep allowing him to steal the hope and joy I have freely given to you? Are you going to allow him to destroy the freedom I purchased for you? My precious children! Stop giving in to him and stretch forth your hands and receive what I have been trying to give to you. I AM willing to restore your hands to receive the goodness I have for you says the Lord (Mark 3:5). Freely receive this day My goodness!!

She saw the pattern.

When things were going well in her life she pushed God aside. When trials came she was searching for Him.

Exodus 8:15 But when Pharaoh saw that there was relief, he hardened his heart and would not listen to Moses and Aaron, just as the LORD had said.

Aaron and Moses were giving Pharaoh the commands to let God's people go and yet Pharaoh was refusing to listen to God's mouthpieces. In doing so, much more hardship fell upon Pharaoh and his kingdom.

What is it that you keep repeating in your life that if you would simply heed to what God is saying would cease? Don't you think it's time to give it up? Isn't it time to listen to ALMIGHTY GOD? Grace has been extended, take the time and repent. He is listening!

Father, forgive us for trying to do it the way we want to. Forgive us for ignoring You and the goodness You have been wanting to bestow upon us. Thank You for Holy Spirit and for putting people in our lives to speak to us. We thank You for Your grace and we repent with all of our hearts in Jesus' name amen.

He had total trust in him.

What was said was what would be done. He took him at his word.

Matthew 8:8 The centurion replied, "Lord, I do not deserve to have you come under my roof. But just say the word, and my servant will be healed.

Have you put more trust in man than you have in what God has said to you? Do you feel unworthy that you think God would not even speak to you where you are at? If so, repent and believe that God is a God that truly loves you so much so that He wants you to take Him at His word and that He considers you worthy to help you!

Psalm 8:3-4 When I consider your heavens, the work of your fingers, the moon and the stars, which you have set in place, what is mankind that you are mindful of them, human beings that you care for them?

Father, we know You are not man that You can lie. We ask forgiveness now for being unfaithful to Your words. We ask now, Father, to knock down those walls that hinder us in taking You at Your words in Jesus' name amen.

She was having a hard time wrapping her mind around what God had just requested from her.

It was exciting yet in the natural it felt daunting.

Matthew 19:26 Jesus looked at them and said, "With man this is impossible, but with God all things are possible."

Has God asked you to do something and you dismissed it because what He told you was so big in your thinking that you simply said "truly there is no way for me to do this!"

God is the maker of the universe so yes, things will seem too big to accomplish in the natural. It's why we always need to lean and depend on Him. Rest easy though, He trusts you and knows you can achieve it.

Remember, no thing is too big for our Almighty God!

Father God, we come now thanking You for who You are! We thank You for the trust You have for us. We ask now, God to rejuvenate that which You spoke to us to accomplish for Your kingdom. We thank You in advance in Jesus' name amen.

He had it all.

A father that loved him greatly. He was loved and trusted deeply that when asked if he could have his fair share of his dads' inheritance his dad it to him.

Yes, he had a good life in the eyes of society and yet he felt he needed to go out and see how much more was out there. He lived to party and flash his money around until it was all gone. He then hit bottom realizing just where he came from. He knew he had better and that this way of living wasn't meant for him. He knew where to come back to.

He had to return to his father and his father's love.

How many of us have pulled away from God believing the world had more to give to just find out we were more empty than ever? No matter what we have done, God is a good daddy waiting for us. Don't let the past dealings keep you in the pig pen, come back home. Get your hearts condition straightened out by Abba Father, He has the best of parties to throw for you!

Luke 15:23-24 Bring the fattened calf and kill it. Let's have a feast and celebrate. For this son of mine was dead and is alive again; he was lost and is found.' So they began to celebrate.

Father, thank You for looking after us, waiting for us to return unto You. Thank You for never throwing our sins up in our face. Thank You for taking us back as Your true sons and daughters. We love You in Jesus' name amen.

He was old and felt time was against him.

When was he to do what God had shown him? At times he questioned whether he had heard God correctly and even at times laughed at what he was told he would do.

Genesis 17:16 I will bless her and will surely give you a son by her. I will bless her so that she will be the mother of nations; kings of peoples will come from her." Abraham fell facedown; he laughed and said to himself, "Will a son be born to a man of hundred years old? Will Sarah bear a child at the age of ninety?"

Father, help us to remember that time is not in our hands but in Yours. Help us to know that it is You that has called things in its time. Forgive us for doubting You and Your ways. Again, forgive us, we pray, for looking in the natural and not in the Spirit. In Jesus' name amen.

Although it was small it had such force behind it.

At times it would bring about blessing and other times it would bring about curses. It is the tongue.

Proverbs 18:21 The tongue has the power of life and death, and those who love it will eat its fruit.

This is such a powerful warning! Either speak good and you will enjoy great results or speak evil and you will reap the negative effects. Yes, this goes even for what we speak over ourselves! We are of The KING of kings and we need to speak as such. Be very mindful of what is produced out of your vessel. You cannot take back words – they will propel you forward.

Yes, we, at times, lose our tempers but in James 1:19 we are told to be quick to hear slow to speak and slow to anger.

Let this be the season that we control our mouthpiece and bring the unity into the church body.

Father, thank You for Your mercy and grace! We come to You for forgiveness for our negative speech whether it be against our brothers and sisters or even ourselves. We ask that our spirit is sensitive to Your correction before we speak. Thank You in Jesus' name amen.

No matter who you are, you will always have seasons in your life.

Some of these seasons are of great joy and other seasons where you feel you are doing good just to put one foot in front of the other. But in all things it's our Heavenly Father that will show His glory we just need to keep pushing through. He knows what we need and what we need to get rid of in our lives. Some may say "this season has been with me for months." You have been thinking that God is mad at you or punishing you but that simply isn't the case. Consider it a great honor that He sees in you that ability to go through. Just quit trying in your own strength.

I was going through a tremendous battle a few years back and I asked Him "what is going on?" (Psalm 86:7). I just felt I couldn't do another day. That's when He showed me a vision that changed my outlook. I was shown a dark, dirty hole and I knew it was damp as well. Then He put a seed in this hole and covered it up. He then showed me the rain and heat that beat down on top of the ground and then that's when I saw it, a green growth that pushed its way through the ground and it kept growing taller and taller. It raised its head and looked up at the sun and opened up into the most beautiful purple flower I have ever seen. By looks this flower was so fragile, dainty to the eye yet He spoke "just as this seed was covered in dampness and darkness encamped around it, it kept growing. It pushed through with all it had within it and it became the flower that I have made it to be. You may feel like you are dying and you can't bear anymore but don't ever think I have left you to fight this alone because I AM here and always will be. You have been called and I have to grow you, mature you."

Whatever it is that you are going through this day, know that you have the Great I AM right beside you!!

In Ecclesiastes 3:1 it reads "To everything there is a season, and a time for every matter or purpose under heaven."

Father, thank You for the goodness You are bringing us into. Thank You for pulling out those issues in our lives that are hindering us. Thank You again for Your unending love in Jesus' name amen.

She saw not only the valleys but also the mountaintops.

Both views were beautiful in their own rights. She knew she would travel to both of these places in her lifetime.

In the moments of our mountain top experiences we show the world our smiles, our laughter etc. It's unfortunate that we, as Christians, also show the world our bitterness in the valley experiences by the grumblings, the negative words and our nasty expressions.

In all things know that it is God Who has sent us these journeys for our good. It shows us when we are in a place of what we deem as distress what needs to be plowed up in our mindsets and in our hearts. Just as a farmer who works the ground before he sows his seed, we need to allow Holy Spirit to work our hearts so that God can plant His goodness in us so that we can bear much fruit.

Those mountaintop experiences are refreshing to our souls. Yet all too often we forget where we have come from. We seem to forget why we are on the mountaintop. It isn't so that we can say "hey world look at me!" No, it's so that we can reach down to those that are where we were to say "it's going to be alright, I've been there and I'm here for you. Give me your hand and let me walk with you. Here is my shoulder, cry if you need to."

While we are on this side of heaven we will visit and revisit the valleys of life but look around when you are there – it's still a lush filled land with green grass and beautiful flowers.

This journey isn't all for naught, no, it's for a greater good. Keep putting one foot in front of the other and keep your eyes upon the one Who sees the greatness that He has put within you! It just may be for you to go through it for the benefit of another.

Proverbs 27:17 As iron sharpens iron, so one person man sharpens another.

Father, help us to see what we need to go through so that we can be beneficial to those around us. Help us with our attitudes in times of trials and help us not to forget You in the mountaintop experiences in Jesus' name amen.

Word of the Lord:

This is the year of the Lord!

Yes, says the Spirit of The Lord, I have been very gracious with you but no flesh will glory in My presence. I will strip away all fleshly motives and ideas and will reveal the true hearts of men. This is a year of renewed faith; a newness of love for Me says the Lord. This is going to be a time of great understanding of who I truly AM! I AM putting a fresh zeal for Me in My people and they are going to know that the yoke has been broken off of their necks. Yes, they are going to breath in Me and not mere man. This newness in Me will reveal great giftings that I have put within My people, new ideas and inventions will come forth from the bonds of men being broken.

My people will have a fresh breath, a fresh wind of revelation for Me that will come only from Me for Me says the Lord! Be ye doers of My word, yes, but for the right reasons – for My glory and no other. If My people are willing, this will be the year for My people for My glory.

AMEN!!

Word of the Lord:

"No longer will My house be a den of thieves. No longer will My name be blasphemed, no longer will you say "this is of the Lord" and it be of mere man. This is the day you are to truly self-examine yourself and come unto me with a repentant heart. My glory is Mine and Mine alone. Who do you think I AM is? Enough! Enough I say!! You have been calling down My glory to come yet you hold yourselves in captivity with your lies! Again, who do you say I AM is?"

He sat in the hay loft with the doors opened wide.

The fresh breeze coupled with the sweet fragrance of the recently baled hay was a scent every country boy, young and old alike, loved. It was a pleasing aroma he could enjoy all the days of his life.

Our prayers, when prayed in sincerity and through and by the name of Jesus, are the same to our heavenly Father. They are a sweet aroma to Him. God takes our prayers very seriously. Do not ever think He doesn't.

Revelation 5:8 And when he had taken it, the four living creatures and the twenty-four elders fell down before the Lamb. Each one had a harp and they were holding golden bowls full of incense, which are the prayers of God's people.

Our Precious Heavenly Father, we thank You for Your listening ears to our prayers. We give thanks that Jesus is making intercession for us daily. We thank You that our prayers are so important to You that You keep them in golden bowls and they are a sweet aroma to You. We thank You for Your love and adoration You have for each of us in Jesus' name amen.

It was enormous in stature.

Breathtaking was its golden yellow and burnt orange leaves. He had always heard of "The Magnificent Oak" but now that he was standing beneath it he was in awe of its unique beauty.

Many a storms had this tree withstood. Winds that would whip right through its branches even at times taking a few down. Rain and snow pelting at its bark, lightening scoring its mark against the tree itself. Seasons of too much rain and yet seasons of drought. Yes, this tree had endured its fair share of many storms; some brutal and others just enough to leave its lasting mark. Nonetheless, it was still standing!

Without a doubt many storms will come up in our lives. Rest assured, they are there to shape and reshape our hearts and our mindsets. Some storms are easy to figure out why we are going through them and others simply have not an explanation. But God has His plan for our lives.

Jeremiah 29:11 "For I know the plans I have for you" declares the LORD, "plans to prosper you and not to harm you, plans to give you hope and a future."

How reassuring is our Heavenly Fathers Words to us! Yes, to prosper and give us hope!

When the clouds are looming over your soul and mind just remember He has us with a great outcome.

Heavenly Father, many times we question the season in our lives. Help us to remember You have us in the palm of Your hand; Your mind is continually on us. We thank You in Jesus' name amen.

Isaiah 49:16 See, I have engraved you on the palms of my hands; your walls are ever before me.

She smiled as she snuggled into her warm blankets.

It felt good, this new freedom she was experiencing. Forgiveness felt great! She could actually breathe and for the first time in a long time she felt life resonating her being.

Unforgiveness hurts those that are holding onto it not those in which have done the wrong deed. Forgiveness is for us. By not forgiving it holds you as prisoner not the other way around. Forgiving isn't saying "you had the right to do..." No, it says "no longer will you exert control over me."

Go ahead, give the enemy of your soul a big black eye and forgive! Forgive and feel life fill you again.

Mark 11:25 And when you stand praying, if you hold anything against anyone, forgive them, so that your Gather in heaven may forgive you your sins."

Praise God for He has forgiven our misdeeds!! Psalm 103:12 as far as the east is from the west, so far has he removed our transgressions from us.

Father, thank You for Your unfailing love. Thank You that when we repent You are faithful and just to forgive us of our sins in Jesus' name amen.

1 John 1:9 If we confess our sins, he is faithful and just and will forgive us our sins and purify us from all unrighteousness.

Word of the Lord:

The Spirit of the LORD says "let it go and watch Me shape you in the way you know your purpose is. Watch and see what I have planned for your life. I say let it go My people just as I ordered to Pharaoh let it go. Let My people go that has hurt you, let the offenses go. Let the disappointments you feel diminish, you are in My hands! I AM is here, I AM has been here and I AM will always be here. Let it go!! Come forth and let Me show you the works of wonders that will be done in you and in your life. Come forth, let it go and watch for I AM is at work" says the LORD!

He stood up wiping the sweat from his brow.

He was downcast and his mind was whirling. Why was it that he, who gave tithes and offerings and helped any he could, was struggling?

He looked around the factory and knew who was a Christian and who wasn't. He knew who just bought a new truck or a bigger house, yet he was the one that was battling. He stopped, prayed and gave thanks that he had peace of mind and Isaiah 48:22 came back to his remembrance and Matthew 6:3-4 that our goods deeds will be rewarded by our Heavenly Father. We need not think that God has forgotten us and yes, in time we will be rewarded with what we have been promised.

Isaiah 48:22 "There is no peace," says the LORD, "for the wicked."

Matthew 6:3-4 But when you give to the needy, do not let your left hand know what your right hand is doing, so that your giving may be in secret. Then your Father, who sees what is done in secret, will reward you.

Heavenly Father we give You all praise in the love You relish upon each of Your children. Help us to remember our deeds are to show Your love to the world in Jesus' name amen.

Hebrews 6:10 God is not unjust; he will not forget your work and the love you have shown him as you have helped his people and continue to help them.

The reunion was bittersweet.

She noticed the ease of their conversations. Not at one point did He have her feeling shamed. Why was it that she thought she had to pull away from Him because of her sins? How sweet their time together had been and the joy she had sitting in His presence. No longer would she distance herself from Him due to her shortcomings.

How often is it that, as Christians, when we sin we hide ourselves from our Heavenly Father? His eyes are always on us even when we fall.

His Word states that He will pardon us, that He won't count our sins against us. It is His delight to forgive us and reconcile us back to Him (2 Cor 5:19). Don't allow your misconceptions of our loving and merciful Father keep you from communing with Him.

Isaiah 43:25 "I, even I, am he who blots out your transgressions, for my own sake, and remembers your sins no more.

Isaiah 55:7 Let the wicked forsake their ways and the unrighteous their thoughts. Let them turn to the LORD, and he will have mercy on them, and to our God, for he will freely pardon.

Father, so many wrong thoughts of You keep Your children from coming to You and soaking in Your love and forgiveness. Change the misconceptions of Your children in Jesus' name amen.

Camouflaged he was able to go undetected walking through the dense woods.

He walked tenderly making sure he wouldn't be noticed approaching his prey for his planned attack.

How this is so with the enemy of our soul. 1 Peter 5:8 Be alert and of sober mind. Your enemy the devil prowls around like a roaring lion looking for someone to devour.

Be alert with the sins of the world trying to pull on you. They will try to keep you distant from The Lover of your soul Christ Jesus.

Loving Father, we sometimes forget that we are in a battle of our hearts and minds. Please help us to guard ourselves and be alert of the enemy in Jesus' name amen.

She stood staring at her reflection.

Her mind went back to her past. She could see herself in ragged clothes. She looked so hopeless and helpless. She saw titles on her reading "thief," "adulteress," "liar," "jealous," "angry," "unloved," "rejected," "hateful."

But now as she looked at herself in her elegant dress she saw herself as "beautiful," "redeemed," "freely forgiven," "child of God," "accepted," "beloved," "lovely," and "chosen."

Isaiah 1:18 "Come, now, let us settle the matter," says the LORD. "Though your sins are like scarlet, they shall be as white as snow; thought they are red as crimson, they shall be like wool.

No longer are we who were in the past once we are redeemed by the Blood of The Lamb! No, we have been made new and we are to see ourselves as such.

2 Corinthians 5:17 therefore, if anyone is in Christ, the new creation has come: The old has gone, the new is here!

Heavenly Father, how blessed we are to have such a good and forgiving Daddy such as you. Thank You for Your love and forgiveness and making us new through Christ Jesus in Jesus' name amen.

She was all nestled in with a mug of steaming hot chocolate.

She watched as the beautiful changing leaves blew off their branches. "Winds of Change" was what she saw.

Ecclesiastes 3:1-8 speaks of time and of things changing and coming to pass. Many fear when their world starts to change but rest assured God will make our paths straight we just need to rely and rest in Him. He is a good daddy and has only the best for us.

Proverbs 3:5-6 Trust in the LORD with all your heart and lean not on your own understanding; in all your ways submit to him and he will make your paths straight.

Father, life is all about changes and for some change is a little overwhelming. Help us to know with our hearts and minds that those changes are not to harm us but are for the good and through all the changes in life we know as Philippians 4:13 states "I can do all this through him who gives me strength" and we give You all praise and honor in Jesus' name amen!

Word of the Lord:

"Seek out those fears and cast them down. Let no fear or bad thoughts keep you at bay. Choose this day to break forth and release the fears of the unknown. Move one step at a time and need not think of the next step until it's time! Where are you putting your trust? Who do you trust? Do you think that asking for bread I would give you a stone? Go forth and rejoice in Me" says the Lord.

Word of the Lord:

For the Spirit of the Lord says "I have prepared a place, a place of refreshing, a place of intimacy for you and Me. In this place you will find My loving arms embracing you. Come now to the place I have prepared and become renewed! Soak in My presence and find the ultimate fulfillment that can only be found in Me. For in Me is joy forever more! Come unto Me and be renewed" says the Lord.

They sat rocking in the night as the moonlight spilled across her little ones face.

She felt the warmth from her child's cheek against her chest.

Ever so preciously her child spoke and said "momma, I hear your heart. It says you love me bunches!"

When was the last time you crawled up in our Heavenly Father's lap and nestled your head against His chest? When was the last time you sat and allowed His tender voice to sing over you?

Zephaniah 3:17 The LORD your God is with you, the Mighty Warrior who saves. He will take great delight in you; in his love he will no longer rebuke you, but will rejoice over you with singing."

Father, we thank you for the praises You sing over each and every one of us. May we take time and sit in stillness to hear the songs You are singing over us. In awe of You, we give thanks to You in Jesus' name amen.

It was dark and the worst storm they had ever been in.

It wasn't the weather for even the most experienced of a yachtsman. They were being thrust about like leaves in a windstorm. It would take a miracle for them to get out of this unharmed.

When we are not grounded in God's Word we are no different than the people in the storm. The enemy of our soul will have a hey-day with our minds and emotions. Let us be grounded in His Word and not believe the lies and false doctrines this world has to offer.

Ephesians 4:14 Then we will no longer be infants, tossed back and forth by the waves, and blown here and there by every wind of teaching and by the cunning and craftiness of people in their deceitful scheming.

Heavenly Father, we humbly come to You asking that You search us. Search us and show where we need to be grounded even more so in You in Jesus' name we pray amen.

His hands are soft to wipe away her tears. His shoulders are strong to carry the weight of the world yet inviting for His little one to ride on. His smile is one of trust. His voice is strong with words of correction but tender to speak words of adoration. His eyes are soft with understanding yet stern to the world with warning. He is of integrity, tenacity and grit. He is a father of love!

Our Father, our heavenly Father, is a perfect example of what pure unadulterated love is about. He reigns with grace, mercy and love; a heart with understanding. His mind is on His beloved children all of the time. Yet, He reigns with righteous judgement. He is a good daddy that we say "Abba Father".

Romans 8:15 The Spirit you received does not make you slaves, so that you live in fear again; rather, the Spirit you received brought about your adoption to sonship. And by him we cry, "Abba, Father."

We are of such great worth to our heavenly Father that He even knows the number of hairs we have! Yes, He is the best daddy one could ever want.

Luke 12:7 Indeed, the very hairs of your head are all numbered. Don't be afraid; you are worth more than many sparrows.

Lean on Him now; sit in His lap with His loving arms around you. Enjoy the everlasting love of The Father!

Heavenly Father, we get so entangled in this earthly life. Those things that do or don't happen to us and we connect them to You. Forgive us Father for not seeing You with the pure love that You have for us. Help us to receive Your love You have for us in Jesus' name amen.

She sat in the quietness reviewing her life.

She wasn't a CEO and had no intentions of being one. She wasn't a board member of a prestigious organization nor was she climbing the corporate ladder of a Fortune 500 company. She wasn't overseas saving third world country people. What she was doing was fulfilling the desires God had put within her.

Too many of us view and grade our lives by what we have accomplished, where we are financially and what we are driving.

We need to have the peace in that which God has called us to and not fulfilling the sinful nature within.

Ephesians 2:10 For we are God's handiwork, created in Christ Jesus to do good works, which God prepared in advance for us to do.

Heavenly Father, we sidestep those paths which You have called us to in order to add more materialistic things to our already crowded lives. Forgive us Father for not seeing what really matters - Your ways. We love You in Jesus' name amen!

They walked hand in hand, at first not speaking, and then it was like an abundant waterfall.

She had so much inside her that had built up. It all came forth gushing like a geyser. He let her tell Him everything that was on her heart and mind. She knew He was intent on hearing her out and what she had to say was important to Him.

How our Heavenly Father wants us to go before Him with all things.

Psalm 28:6-9 Praise be to the LORD, for he has heard my cry for mercy. The LORD is my strength and my shield; my heart trusts in him, and he helps me. My heart leaps for joy, and with my song I praise him.

Father, how You care for Your children in every aspect. Help us to lean into this understanding in Jesus' name amen.

Word of the Lord:

"For I have come for the broken heart and heavy-laden. For I have come to set the captives free. For I have come to bring you peace in mind and spirit. I have come to clothe the soul in sweet peace and love. I AM the honeycomb. I AM the refreshing waters to your dry and parched lives. I AM the way maker when you can't find your ways. I AM your everlasting and true love. I AM He who wants to bear your problems, your concerns. I AM He who wants to hear your hearts cries and desires. Yes, I AM He who never leaves you nor could ever want to. Yes, I AM He who satisfies you. Now! Now come unto Me and share all with Me. I have much to say and many Words of adoration for you. Come unto ME and see. Come unto Me and hear My precious ones!"

He stood staring at the headstone.

He knew for awhile that time was short and he would be saying his good-byes. This was a death that he was at peace with and willingly embraced.

It was a death unto himself; a death to the mindsets of not feeling forgiven, of unworthiness. He stood and drank in a deep breath of the mercy and grace that has been extended to him by his heavenly Father.

Psalm 116:5 The LORD is gracious and righteous; our God is full of compassion.

Your Word Father is pure sweetness to a soul in need. We thank You Lord for Your mercies that You willingly extend. Help us loving Father to embrace them in Jesus' name amen!

She stood with her hands on her hips.

"But I don't want just one, I want all of them!"

She wasn't being ungrateful for what she was given; she simply wasn't going to settle for anything less.

Psalm 37:4 Take delight in the LORD, and he will give you the desires of your heart.

Mark 11:24 Therefore I tell you, whatever you ask for in prayer, believe that you have received it, and it will be yours.

Are you delighting yourself in God and believing Him and His Word for that which you are asking for? How are you viewing heavenly Father?

Father, You have all in the palm of Your hands. Your love for us is unending and by You comes the desires within our hearts. Help us to believe and receive that which You have for us in Jesus' name amen!

She was putting the final puzzle piece in.

This had been a long but joyous and fulfilling 15,000 piece puzzle that she had worked on. Every piece designed for its specific position.

How true we are in the Body of Christ. Each and every one of us designed for His specific purpose. We may not like someone's personality but rest assured they have been personally designed by The Creator Himself for His purposes.

Ephesians 2:10 For we are God's handiwork, crated in Christ Jesus to do good works, which God prepared in advance for us to do.

Psalm 139:14 I praise you because I am fearfully and wonderfully made; your works are wonderful, I know that full well.

Father, if only we could truly get the understanding not just in our mind but into our spirit that Your people belong to You and Your ways not ours. Each of us designed for Your purposes and not for ours. Help us to love and accept them the way You do in Jesus' name amen!

She took the rag across the dirty pane and was awestruck.

She could not have imagined what beauty lay hidden under the many years of dirt and grime.

She climbed down from the ladder and stood staring at the splendor in the stained glass window. So breathtakingly beautiful was the way in which the light reflected its beauty.

1 John 1:7 But if we walk in the light, as he is in the light, we have fellowship with one another, and the blood of Jesus, his Son, purifies us from all sin.

1 Corinthians 6:11 And that is what some of you were. But you were washed, you were sanctified, you were justified in the name of the LORD Jesus Christ and by the Spirit of our God.

Father, so many of us think we cannot or should not be used by You due to issues of our past. We need to just rest in Your hands knowing You have washed us clean and Your beauty shines through us for Your glory.

The road was a long and rough journey.

It was arduous and exhausting. Every movement had to be made with extreme movements and every fiber of his being felt it yet he had the finish line in sight.

In this life we will, without a doubt, go through some tough times. In these times our very core of who we are and what we believe will be shaken. In these times we must stand on God's Word and in doing so we hold on to His peace that only He can give. We will be sustained by the Very One who loves us.

2 Corinthians 8-9 We are hard pressed on every side, but not crushed; perplexed, but not in despair; persecuted, but not abandoned; struck down, but not destroyed.

Father, those times in which we are pressed on every side help us to hold fast to You, the One we know that we know will hold on to us. We love You and we praise You in Jesus' name amen.

The setting was peaceful not only to her mind but to her spirit as well.

As she sat and observed the coming and going of the ocean water she started noticing an exchange going on with each flow.

The water was depositing yet it would also take something with it as it drew back.

This is how God works in our lives. He wants to make a deposit of peace, joy and happiness as we relinquish out our fears, worries and attitudes.

1 Peter 5:7 Cast all your anxiety on him because he cares for you.

Psalm 55:22 Cast your cares on the LORD and he will sustain you; he will never let the righteous be shaken

Father, we cast all our cares upon You for it is by and through You we obtain the victory. We thank You that Your eye is upon us as we come and go in Jesus' name amen.

Psalm 33:18 But the eyes of the LORD are on those who fear him, on those whose hope is in his unfailing love

She wanted it to be a gift like no other.

It wasn't that she thought it had to be an expensive gift but one that only she could give. It was a gift from her heart and so she poured out her heart to Him.

Psalm 51:17 My sacrifice, O God, is a broken spirit; a broken and contrite heart you, God, will not despise.

Father, why do we think we can hide the truth from You when in fact You simply want us in how we are? Your Word is simple, to give You our broken selves. Help us to walk in this truth in Jesus' name amen!

There it was nestled in the midst of all the thorns, the perfect rose holding its beauty.

She studied it and its placement in its life; surrounded by the very thing that could protect it or the very thing that could destroy it.

This is how waiting on our Lord is. While in the midst of our waiting we can patiently rest in His hands or we can push in our own ways destroying that which is meant for us to watch and grow in. For in this holding pattern we can know our Heavenly Father is still at work in our lives.

Psalm 27:14 Wait on the LORD: be strong and take heart and wait for the LORD.

Father, we get so impatient with the things in life. We seem to get caught up in looking for the completed work that we don't see the beauty in the time of waiting. Help us to not lose heart and keep our focus on You in Jesus' name amen.

She felt relaxed as she hadn't in months.

She took in a cleansing breath and exhaled with the songs of praise and adoration she had for her Heavenly Father. Yes, she was resting in Him.

Matthew 11:28-30 "Come to me, all you who are weary and burdened, and I will give you rest. Take my yoke upon you and learn from me, for I am gentle and humble in heart, and you will find rest for your souls. For my yoke is easy and my burden is light."

Father, forgive us for walking in self-sufficiency trying to work in our own strengths and not by Yours. Help us to realize when we are doing this in Jesus' name amen.

He looked out his tractor window rubbing his chin.

He knew some of the land was as hard as a rock. Other parts of the field were going to work up very tenderly; how this is the condition of our hearts. Some areas are easy for us to surrender unto God to work on while others are not as pleasant.

Matthew 15:18-19 But the things that come out of a person's mouth come from the heart, and these defile them. For out of the heart come evil thoughts—murder, adultery, sexual immorality, theft, false testimony, slander.

Father, how we desire to bring You glory in our lives. Open our eyes Lord; show us where we need to allow You to plow up those areas in our hearts. We love You Father and we thank You in Jesus' name amen.

"Come out, come out wherever you are!" was the child's hearty cry.

Playing hide and seek was their game of choice and they enjoyed the hunt.

Isn't this God's proclamation to us? "Come out of your hiding, come out from your sins, and come out from your insecurities and shame! Come out, come out and come unto Me!"

Lay your issues, those that you want resolved and yes, even those you would rather ignore, at the Lord's feet. He is calling us up and out and has already made our way straight.

Genesis 3:9 But the LORD God called to the man, "Where are you?"

Father, You love us deeply and dearly and want only the best for us. Your glory shines in the unending forgiveness You freely give us. Thank You Abba Father for Your love in Jesus' name amen!

The tears wouldn't stop flowing.

She lay with her hair and pillow wet from the endless tears. She thought by now the pain would have left but it seemed at times that it was intensified.

Isaiah 53:4, "Surely he hath borne our griefs, and carried our sorrows: yet we did esteem him stricken, smitten of God, and afflicted."

Psalm 147:3 He heals the brokenhearted and binds up their wounds

Father, You love us and nothing can change that, we thank You! Father, we ask that we hold on to the truth that You care of every area in our lives and that the work Christ did on Calvary's cross is for our emotional healings as well. We thank You in Jesus' name amen.

He was holding on.

Those around him were speaking words of despair. He needed to hear words of encouragement and nobody was speaking them. Yet when he wanted to simply give up he would dig deep within and revert to God's Word.

Psalm 119:50 My comfort in my suffering is this: Your promise preserves my life.

Father, when we are going through life's curveballs help us to hold on to Your promises. Your Word does not fail and we know that we know You cannot lie. Through it all Lord, Job held on and we need to as well. Thank You Father in Jesus' name amen.

Numbers 23:19 God is not a man, that he should lie, nor a son of man, that he should change his mind. Does he speak and then not act? Does he promise and not fulfill?

Hebrews 6:18 God did this so that, by two unchangeable things in which it is impossible for God to lie, we who have fled to take hold of the hope offered to us may be greatly encouraged.

She lay with her fragile hands on her children's.

The prognosis wasn't delightful to her children yet she had a warm smile and excitement in her eyes.

As her children were asking her of her desires she enthusiastically stated "you can have my world just give me Jesus!"

Matthew 16:26 What good will it be for someone to gain the whole world, yet forfeit their soul? Or what can anyone give in exchange for their soul?

Father, how blessed we are to call You our daddy! Help us to keep our focus on what truly counts. For Lord, we don't discount the blessings You have given and those that we have coming but Lord, we need to keep things in perspective. We love You in Jesus' name amen.

Matthew 6:33 But seek first his kingdom and his righteousness, and all these things will be given to you as well.

The sight was breathtaking.

The bird was majestic as well as beautiful. The ease in which the eagle soared looked so effortlessly yet powerful.

Isaiah 40:31 but those who hope in the LORD will renew their strength. They will soar on wings like eagles; they will run and not grow weary, they will walk and not be faint.

Father, when we rest in You we find life to be easier. Easier to walk the walk, easier to enjoy the days You've put before us. Easier to come to You and praise You. Help us Father to hold on to a different perspective so that we can mount up and soar in this life. We thank You in Jesus' name amen.

Exodus 19:4 'You yourselves have seen what I did to Egypt, and how I carried you on eagles' wings and brought you to myself.

How her heart ached!

She confided in her because she was led to do so. Instead of an understanding word or a loving embrace she was met with a smug look.

How could her loved one give this terrible reaction to what she was going through? As if she were glad she had this turmoil going on.

1 Thessalonians 5:11 Therefore encourage one another and build each other up, just as in fact you are doing.

Father, how sad of a situation but Lord, help us to see the problem resides within them yet keep us looking within ourselves to learn and be careful that this sin isn't knocking on our doorstep. So much love for You in Jesus' name amen!

1 Corinthians 13:4-7

It was exhilarating!

The brightly colored kite soaring in the sky. It would go higher then dive down then up, up, up again.

Luke 17:5 The apostles said to the Lord, "Increase our faith!"

Father, watching a kite is relevant to our faith. We have our up and down moments. Circumstances happen; some instances might make us weak in faith while other challenges might build our faith quickly. Help us Father, to realize in the end it all strengthens us. We pray in Jesus' name amen.

Go, Stop, Yield, Do Not Enter, One Way, Caution...; so many ways yet so many hindrances.

Which way was he to go or which way was he not to go? His mind was wheeling with fear of making the wrong decision. He was afraid of what was to come yet he knew he had to make a move.

This is so true in life in doing what God has called us to. It seems we second guess every move because of fear. Fear of the unknown, fear of the path not being familar, fear of making mistakes. Rest assured, if we just put one foot in front of the other God will direct our steps.

Proverbs 3:5-7 Trust in the LORD with all your heart and lean not on your own understanding; in all your ways submit to him, and he will make your paths straight.

Just as Mary was told that she found great favor with God and to not be afraid we too should be assured that if God has called us to it we have found favor with God.

Luke 1:28 The angel went to her and said, "Greetings, you who are highly favored! The LORD is with you."

Father, help us to walk the walk You have put before us. Help us to realize You have our paths before us. Help us Father to not rely upon ourselves but You and Your ways in Jesus' name amen.

He wasn't ignoring the call.

He heard his name but couldn't figure out where or who was calling for him.

Then he heard, he heard with clarity and found his friend in the midst of the crowd.

John 10:27 My sheep listen to my voice; I know them, and they follow me.

Father, in all of the chaos around us help us to hear You. You calling out to us to come rest, dine and listen to Your voice amongst all that is battling for our attention. It is Your voice that calls us to peace, love, mercy, grace and repentance. We thank You Father, we thank You for calling us unto You in Jesus' name amen.

1 Samuel 3:4 Then the LORD called Samuel. Samuel answered, "Here I am."

There he stood; his cape flowing in the wind and his plastic sword in hand.

He was going to slay the enemies that came his way and he was proud to be a warrior!

How true this should be for us Christians. Proud to stand tall against the enemy and blessed to be called to the battles in life. Unfortunately, we sometimes grumble of the lessons we are to learn and shriek in the face of our "Goliaths" in life.

Father, we pray that we will be as David, eager to go to war with those raging issues and fight the enemy of our soul. Help us to remember Father; it is by You that we have our strength. Help us Father to battle for those around us and not only for ourselves in Jesus' name amen.

1 Samuel 17:47 All those gathered here will know that it is not by sword or spear that the LORD saves; for the battle is the LORD's, and he will give all of you into our hands.

He studied and then gave a smirk.

He thought he was going to say "king me" until he went to move his checker. Doing so, he realized he had made an illegal move and was beat at his own game.

This is the truth with the enemy of our souls. He thinks he has us cornered and beat but when we have Jesus he can't win. He has lost his hand against the Blood and name of Jesus Christ. The victory of the Cross is victory for us!

1 Corinthians 15:57 But thanks be to God! He gives us the victory through our Lord Jesus Christ.

Abba Father, thank You! Thank You for Your Son going to the Cross for all healings, burdens, diseases, afflictions, death. Again, thank You for Your endless love. We pray in the most precious and holy name Jesus amen!

Word of the Lord:

"I say that You are My sons & daughters, that I love you, that I adore you, that I need your communion as you need Mine. I say that our relationship needs more communication. I say that I need to hear your heart and I need you to know you can trust Me. Now you need to know all this as well and you need to know I know all but want to hear it all from you. Why sit and think that you need to carry all by yourself says the Lord? I AM is not far but ever so near. I AM is a good daddy that wants such a relationship with you and you need to know this and not be afraid. You need to know that I hear you and yes, I AM here to respond, intervene and show you things. You need to glean from these moments and not fret. You need to come to Me more and less of you. Relationship is built on trust, honor and respect; openness from heart to heart and a listening spirit. You know deep within that I have it taken care of you just need not listen to the voices of doubt. Learn of Me and from Me. I have much to share and teach. I love for My children to hear My heart not just for themselves but for others. My heart bled when My Son bled for My people and I still feel that day. I still call My people to Me" says the Lord, "I still long for them to come dine with Me daily not just when they feel like it. I want them to have such a deep and burning desire to worship Me and let them see it change their lives. I AM love and I AM is in love with My people. I call them Mine" says the Lord, "I call them redeemed and glorified through My Son and they need to get this understanding in their very being. I AM in love with My creation and desire My creation to come unto Me now" says the Lord. "I AM never changing I have seen from beginning to end and rejoice for the victories are yours forever more. Come, partake of My goodness and listen to Me, My heart. I AM has much to say! Come now, dine with Me, lets talk, share, commune, lets rejoice for the victories at hand, come now My child and rejoice!"

It was made from her heart.

Although she was not an artist it did not stop her from creating. It was beautiful in its own simplicity. The bowl was not a standard of perfection but a bowl of love.

2 Corinthians 10:12 We do not dare to classify or compare ourselves with some who commend themselves. When they measure themselves by themselves and compare themselves with themselves, they are not wise.

Father, how we find amazement in all You have made. You haven't called us to be perfect but righteous by the blood and name of Jesus. In this crazy world where it seems that we should measure up one to another help us to put that notion down and pick up Your love and that You created us with Your very hands and breath. We love You in Jesus' name amen!

She bent down to pick up the pieces.

The now broken heirloom that had been passed down for many generations lay in many pieces.

She turned a piece over in her hand and saw a way to repurpose all the pieces. It would be beautiful in a new way.

2 Corinthians 5:17 Therefore, if anyone is in Christ, the new creation has come: The old has gone, the new is here!

Father, we give You that which you want, all those issues that You want to mend, heal and bring forth. We look forward to the new while giving up our old in Jesus' name amen!!

Isaiah 43:19 See, I am doing a new thing! Now it springs up; do you not perceive it? I am making a way in the wilderness and streams in the wasteland.

She had all the ingredients laid out and one by one she added them to her bowl.

Stir, mix, sift and beat; it was all to be done to get to the finished product.

It was a process but one that she knew would be worth it.

How this is in our lives with God our Father. Some things have to be added, some things have to be combined and other things beaten and sifted but all so that we can become a better us for God's glory.

Matthew 3:12 His winnowing for is in his hand, and he will clear his threshing floor, gathering his wheat into the barn and burning up the chaff with unquenchable fire.

Father, we thank You for the process we have to go through. Many times we kick and scream throughout the process but we ultimately know it will benefit us for Your kingdom in Jesus' name amen.

They walked hand in hand singing "Glory to the Lamb."

Although they were with each other they were praising God as though they were alone.

They had encouraged and built the other up in the Lord and praise sprung forth within their hearts.

1 Thessalonians 5:11 Therefore encourage one another and build each other up, just as in fact you are doing.

Father, just as Your Word says to build one another up it has a residual effect in our own lives. Father, building one up brings our ownselves up in You. Father, how awesome it is to see Your works spring forth in so many ways! All this we pray in Jesus' name amen.

She walked up the overgrown path.

Memories came flooding back to her as one foot went in front of the other.

How she could remember her soul feeling as the old house looked.

Window panes broken just as her soul felt broken. The front door barely hanging on to the frame as if it had been her mind trying to hold on to some sanity. The roof caving as though it were her heart heavy with grief. It was the house Satan had built.

Within time God had constructed a new life within, a place of peace and hopefulness; a place of serenity. Because she gave her life to God He was building a beautiful home.

1 Peter 2:5 You also, like living stones, are being built into a spiritual house to be a holy priesthood, offering spiritual sacrifices acceptable to God through Jesus Christ.

Father, we come asking You to rebuild our house. Come in and repair that which the enemy has tried to overtake. Repair those places God, in which have been hit with despair, curses and all other foul things. Help us to see Father, the great work that is being done in Jesus' precious name amen!

Word of the Lord:

"You who say I AM the Great I Am why do you worry. Do you not see that My hand covers you? That I AM has you covered in every seasons of your lives whether it be of good report or not. Do you not see that in these trials I AM is working those issues out whether it be of fear, stress or pride? Do not think I AM has left you to yourselves but know I AM still and will always have you in the palm of MY hand" says the Lord. "Stand tall and stand secure in Me that all is for a purpose. I have not nor will I ever leave you" says the Lord "and that is a sure Word that you can always count on. You who says I AM the Great I AM, who AM I in your lives? In these seasons that stretch you let it be shown who you really think I AM is. Know this, I AM is a faithful and awesome daddy; a daddy who loves you beyond your concept of what faithful and awesome is. Stand tall in the seasons of adversity and come even closer to Me and I will show Myself Faithful and True. Do not lean to your misguided illustrations but see that which is True. True and Faithful is HE Who has you" says the Lord.

He stood with fear gripping him.

On the outside he seemed composed but within he was a nervous wreck.

It was all the "what-ifs" going through his mind. His focus was going to the negative instead of holding on to His promises.

Matthew 14:28-31 "Lord, if it's you," Peter replied, "tell me to come to you on the water." "Come," he said. Then Peter got down out of the boat, walked on the water and came toward Jesus. But when he saw the wind, he was afraid and, beginning to sink, cried out, "Lord save me!" Immediately Jesus reached out his hand and caught him. "You of little faith," he said, "why did you doubt?"

Father, how we may wake with sound faith and as the day goes on we take our focus off of You. Help us to set our sights on You continually. Thank You Father for Your unending love in Jesus' name amen.

It was a stunning sight!

So many different colored butterflies all feasting on the delicate flowers.

The small flowers giving nourishment to each butterfly fulfilling what they had need off.

Jeremiah 15:16 When your words came, I ate them; they were my joy and my heart's delight, for I bear your name, LORD God Almighty.

Psalm 119:103 How sweet is your words to my taste, sweeter than honey to my mouth!

Father, how sweet it is to dine on Your Words You have given to us. Help us dear Lord, to keep them near and dear to us and not forsake You and Your ways in this life we live. We thank You Father for the nectar You have for us to draw upon. With grateful hearts we pray in Jesus' name amen.

It was all the nay - sayers and the doom and gloom talks.

It was the negativity constantly being in her ear. At times she felt as though she was in a tug-of-war match for her faith.

Isaiah 26:4 Trust in the LORD forever, for the LORD, the LORD himself, is the Rock eternal.

Father, we know Your Words are faithful. We know there is only truth in You. Help us Father to block out all the noise around to keep us close to You. Let our anchor be You Abba! Help us to not be tossed this way and the other (Ephesians 4:14). We give all praise to You in Jesus' precious name amen!

She sat on the bridge feet dangling taking in the beautiful countryside all around her.

She watched as the water took its course.

She could only think how her loving God has always had her in His hand in every course of her life.

She worshipped the One who continually has her.

Job 12:10 In his hand is the life of every creature and the breath of all mankind.

Father, is there any words that can express the love You have for us? All pale in comparison to Who You are. Father, we thank You for having us continually in Your hand in the beautiful name of Jesus amen.

He stood firm and said "no thanks."

The rain pouring down even harder with the thought in his head he should have taken the man's offer of the umbrella.

Instead there he stood wet and cold to the bone.

Hebrews 4:16 Let us then approach God's throne of grace with confidence, so that we may receive mercy and find grace to help us in our time of need.

Father, how many times have You extended Your hand of grace and we've ignored it or thought we were undeserving? Father, we are deserving because of that which Your Son, Jesus Christ, laid down His life for. Forgive us and help us to receive that which has been given to us in Jesus' name amen.

The view was breathtaking.

The sun was rising with awe-inspiring colors that were painting the sky.

She noticed that the more the sun rose the more peace she had.

Colossians 3:1 Since, then, you have been raised with Christ, set your hearts on things above, where Christ is, seated at the right hand of God.

Romans 15:33 The God of peace be with you all. Amen.

Father, when Christ rose from the grave we arose with Him. In that rising came the peace, joy and love that only You can give. Thank You Lord, that with nature we can see You and Your love. In such awe we pray in Jesus' name amen.

"My God, my God why have I forsaken You?"

It was a question she heard in her own thinking.

She knew that her God would not ever forsake her because she believed Him and His Word but yet she knew herself.

Luke 15:20 So he got up and went to his father. But while he was still a long way off, his father saw him and was filled with compassion for him; he ran to his son, threw his arms around him and kissed him."

Father, why is it we pull away, we withdraw unto ourselves instead of running full tilt to Your loving arms? Thank You for those moments in which You allow us to hear You so that we can realign to Your embrace. Thank You for accepting us back! With thankful hearts we pray in Jesus' name amen.

It was a tender moment between them.

They walked hand in hand speaking words of love between them, words of adoration.

There they stood now facing each other. She looked up and spoke "daddy, I love you so much!" He smiled and with arms stretched wide said, "My child, I love you this much!" Sunlight piercing through His nail scarred hands.

John 3:16 For God so loved the world that he gave his one and only Son, that whoever believes in him shall not perish but have eternal life.

Psalm 94:1 For the LORD will not reject his people; he will never forsake his inheritance."

Precious Father, how You love us. How You see the greatness You have put within and how You never give up on any of us. Thank You Father for Your perfect and unfailing love in Jesus' name amen.

She fell and she fell hard.

He extended His hand to her pulling her up and into His gentle, assuring embrace.

He then bent down and dusted her off and cleansed her wounds. All the while telling her all is well. She couldn't help but to believe His words and the tender love He spoke toward her.

Psalm 145:14 The LORD upholds all who fall and lifts up all who are bowed down.

Father, there are times when we simply fall from Your ways. Your love that picks us up and reassures us that we are still loved by You and that Your grace and mercy is continually there for us. Thank You Father for Your beautiful love in Jesus' name amen.

It was his constant companion.

Everywhere he went his little stuffed bear went as well.

That little bear was his side-kick, his friend and his comfort when all was scary around him.

2 Corinthians 1:3-4 Praise be to the God and Father of our Lord Jesus Christ, the Father of compassion and the God of all comfort, who comforts us in all our troubles, so that we can comfort those in any trouble with the comfort we ourselves receive from God.

Father, help us to grab ahold of You as our constant companion. Help us to rely on You when things are well and when things seem scary in our world. You gave us Holy Spirit to be our Comforter (John 14:16) and for that we thank You in Jesus' name amen.

She noticed her foot tapping.

Then her hands started clapping. Before long she was moving across the floor dancing to the heavenly tune in her head.

She even felt a smile across her face. Oh, so long it seemed that she had this joy.

Psalm 30:11-12 You turned my wailing into dancing; you removed my sackcloth and clothed me with joy, that my heart may sing your praises and not be silent. Lord my God, I will praise you forever.

Father, help us to hold on to the spirit of praise when life is down. Help us Lord to continually praise You in all seasons of life. In Jesus' name we pray amen.

It was a one-way road.

One traveling needed to simply breathe in the beauty.

It had many twists and turns, hills and valleys but there was something so serene in it all.

John 14:6 Jesus answered, "I am the way and the truth and the life. No one comes to the Father except through me."

Father, You are our one way road. In this quest of life we are to trust in You through the twists and turns and the ups and downs. You Father are Truth and Life. In all of this when we rest in You we will find this travel to be serene. Excitement waiting around the bend instead of fear. Thank You for holding our hands, thank You for holding our hearts and thank You for the steadiness You give us when we are unsure. Thank You Father in Jesus' name amen.

She sat slumped in her chair.

There was a war going on within her and she knew not what to do.

Then with determination she stood and faith rose within her.

2 Chronicles 20:17 "You will not have to fight this battle. Take up your positions; stand firm and see the deliverance the LORD will give you, Judah and Jerusalem. Do not be afraid; do not be discouraged. Go out to face them tomorrow, and the LORD will be with you.'"

Father, thank You for Your deliverance in the trials and temptations we have to face in this life. Thank You for being with us always in Jesus' name we pray amen.

Word of the Lord:

"For I have called you into the season of cleansing" says the Lord. "Do not shrink back. Instead brace My hands as I do this new thing. My child, I have your heart. Your heart is in My hands. You may think it is breaking but know this, it's My ways and they are good. This is a season of rejuvenation, refreshing and yes, a season of new things. Do not shrink back because it feels foreign or hurtful. There's a breaking going on led by Me. Come now My precious one and let us walk this together. Know I AM is a good daddy. Know this is a season of greatness" says the Lord.

She could not believe it!

Although covered in dirt and having gone through many storms and seasons it was still beautiful.

She found her antique ring she had lost in her flower garden.

Father, we ourselves have seasons in which we go through. Some seasons we get dirty and other seasons we get cleansed. You know what is needed to get us closer to You. Through it all Lord You have us. You see the beauty that is there and we thank You for Your perfect ways in Jesus' name amen.

1 Peter 1:6 In all this you greatly rejoice, though now for a little while you may have had to suffer grief in all kinds of trials.

It was the most amazing sight.

The waterfall was electrifying. The force of the water was that of cleansing yet the flow seemed so tender and the depth was endless.

Ephesians 3:16-19 I pray that out of his glorious riches he may strengthen you with power through his Spirit in your inner being, so that Christ may dwell in your hearts through faith. And I pray that you, being rooted and established in love, may have power, together with all the Lord's holy people, to grasp how wide and long and high and deep is the love of Christ, and to know this love that surpasses knowledge—that you may be filled to the measure of all the fullness of God."

Father, oh Father! Your love is a waterfall and Your grace and mercy beyond expression. Father, help us to embrace Your love, Your amazing love in Jesus' name amen.

Word of the Lord:

"My beautiful and precious child! My hand is outstretched. I long for you to freely take hold and walk this path. I AM is here and near. Oh, if My beloved children would truly understand My love and the depth that I walk with them fear and intimidation would be a very minute thing in their lives. My child, look, look up for your Redemption is here. Oh My precious one, how I love you to the depths of all depths. My love cannot be won nor can it be lost. Hold My hand My beautiful one and let us walk this together. Know this My child, I have you" says the Lord "and I AM will not nor never let go"

Father, we ourselves have seasons in which we go through. Some seasons we get dirty and other seasons we get cleansed. You know what is needed to get us closer to You. Through it all Lord You have us. You see the beauty that is there and we thank You for Your perfect ways in Jesus' name amen.

1 Peter 1:6 In all this you greatly rejoice, though now for a little while you may have had to suffer grief in all kinds of trials.

Word of the Lord:

"Contend for those things we've spoken about. Line your ways with Mine and watch extreme progress happen. Dust off the prophecies that have been spoken and speak and believe them again. I AM is not man therefore I cannot and will not lie. Bring to Me the issues that have been brought to your attention. Do not for a moment hold them close. These are Mine" says the Lord. "Do not think I AM has forgotten you. I could never forget you My beautiful one, no, never!! Speak to the winds of change and see things happen" says the Lord "and watch, watch out for things are happening!"

She bent down.

She ran her hand in the heaps of ashes that were before her.

Gone in an instant was what she had known. Now she knew there was to be a fresh start. It didn't lessen the pain or grief but within her was a refreshing rain being poured over her spirit. With this she had hope springing forth.

Isaiah 61:3 and provide for those who grieve in Zion— to bestow on them a crown of beauty instead of ashes, the oil of joy instead of mourning, and a garment of praise instead of a spirit of despair. They will be called oaks of righteousness, a planting of the Lord for the display of his splendor.

Father, Your beautiful Word promises us that You will give us beauty for our ashes. Father, thank You for Your promises in Jesus' name amen.

Word of the Lord:

"There are pearls before you. Take the pieces and you will see that each of these beautiful pearls are attached to another. I have put these strands of pearls before you so that you can see the beauty that is before you. Just as a pearl is in the dark no less it is still there. I've had your hand and I still have it My child. You are not to see in the natural but see in the supernatural and the natural will be revealed. Go forth and know, know without a doubt I have you" says the Lord.

She finally noticed the growth of the weeds. How could they have gotten out of hand?

In life our wrong desires are like weeds. They grow and before too long they have consumed us.

James 1:14-15 but each person is tempted when they are dragged away by their own evil desire and enticed. Then, after desire has conceived, it gives birth to sin; and sin, when it is full-grown gives birth to death.

Father, some things are so noticeable and some things are so subtle that come into our lives. Show us this day Father, desires that are dangerous. Thank You for Your unending love and patience in Jesus' name amen.

Before she knew it she had devoured 2 of the tasty cinnamon rolls.

Sin is the same way. One bite becomes two and on and on it goes.

It's that little thought, that wrong attitude and even the wrong perception that will grow within you if not taken care of. Repentance should be daily. After all, we are still on this side of heaven!

God's love and forgiveness is like the sweet icing over those rolls or that honey butter on that fresh, hot loaf of bread. It makes it even tastier!

Psalm 34:8 Taste and see the LORD is good; blessed is the one who takes refuge in him.

Father, You are so delightful to our souls! We thank You for Your forgiveness when we come asking for it. We thank You for Your gentle, loving hands that hold us close when we repent. Thank You Father for Your love in Jesus' name amen.

The hurt was as venomous as a snake's bite.

He knew he would have to shake it off and quickly before it became deadly.

What has bitten you in life? Has someone bitten you with words or actions? Has life bitten you with its cycles of trials? If so, are you going to shake it off or are you going to let it keep itself attached to you?

Acts 28:5 But Paul shook the snake off into the fire and suffered no ill effects.

James 4:7 Submit yourselves to God. Resist the devil, and he will flee from you.

Father, forgive us for taking the bites in life and hanging on to them instead of shaking them off. Forgive us for hurting those in our lives as well. We ask You for Your anointing oil to pour over these wounds in life. We choose to shake off these issues all for Your glory in Jesus' name amen.

She stood staring.

She knew she was to move forward. Seeing what was in front of her she simply didn't know how.

Father, when we have mountains or waters that seem to make our next move look impossible help us to see that we need to grab a hold of Your hand. You have our paths already set before us. Trust is key and we need to rely on what we know - that You have us. We pray in Jesus' name amen.

Isaiah 41:13 NIV "For I am the Lord your God who takes hold of your right hand and says to you, Do not fear; I will help you."

It was stagnant waters.

Nothing flowing in and nothing flowing out. The stench of it all was unbearable.

John 7:38 "Whoever believes in me, as Scripture has said, rivers of living water will flow from within them."

Father, when we stop communing with Holy Spirit, when we stop praying, interceding and believing Your word we become like stagnant waters. Help us Father to keep the living waters flowing in our lives - You! In Jesus' name amen

About the Author

Sharisse Elaine (Robinson) Arnold was born November 29, 1974.

Born and raised in rural Indiana she has enjoyed country living.

Married to her husband Brandon and together raising their 2 daughters, Elaney and Kinlee, she has seen God's hand on her life in many amazing ways. Sharisse has a desire for all to come to the saving knowledge of Jesus Christ.

Printed in the United States
By Bookmasters